Beautiful on Land,

Lovely in the Air,

But Birds of the Water,

Of all are most Fair.

Anonymous

ANHINGA

▲ The Anhinga does not have oil glands for waterproofing his feathers like most water birds. When he goes swimming, his feathers get wet. This helps him dive and chase fish under water. But, above water, he must spread his wings to dry in the sun. He can fly with wet feathers, but not as well. Also, it must be too cold to stay wet.

The beautiful white wing feathers are the plumage of the adult. The long tail has given the Anhinga another nickname, "Water Turkey." Because of his jerking swimming motions, he is also called a "Darter."

▲ The female Anhinga is easy to spot. Her neck and chest feathers are much lighter in color than the male.

The Anhinga likes shallow fresh water ponds, streams, and swampy areas rather than coastal beaches.

Immature Anhinga
(Threat Display)

▲ The long powerful neck gives the Anhinga tremendous striking force for spearfishing. The odd looking twist in the neck is due to the position of the neck bones.

1. Look out below! This Anhinga's hungry and on the prowl for dinner. The fish should be worried, with such a skilled fisherman at work.

2. Got him! This photo also shows why the Anhinga is sometimes called "Snakebird." When swimming, his body is completely submerged, with only his neck above the water.

3. The Anhinga spears his prey with his pointed beak like an arrow shot from a bow. Sometimes the spear thrust is so powerful that the Anhinga has to swim to shore and pry the fish off his beak by rubbing it against a rock.

4. The fish, once free of the beak, is flipped into the air and swallowed head first. The size of the fish captured and eaten ranges from "small" to "unbelievable."

CORMORANTS
Double-crested Cormorant

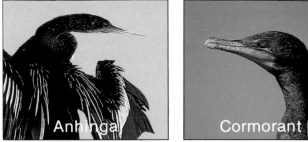

Anhinga

Cormorant

Cormorant versus Anhinga

Cormorants and Anhingas are frequently confused. They are both black birds that dive under the water to fish. Both must dry their feathers in the sun.

The differences are easy to see. The Anhinga's beak is *pointed* for spearing fish, while the Cormorant's beak is *hooked* for grasping its prey. The Cormorant's body remains above the surface when swimming. It lacks the Anhinga's slender neck, long tail, and white wing feathers.

There are many different types of cormorants worldwide. The type found in Florida is called the "Double-crested" Cormorant because of small tufts of feathers that appear on the head during the breeding season.

Oriental Slave Labor

In the Far East, the Cormorant's fishing ability is harnessed for man. The owner of a flock of Cormorants will place metal rings around the birds' necks and place them on leashes. Each bird is released from a small boat and dives to catch fish.

The ring prevents the bird from swallowing. Bird and fish are reeled in together and the fish confiscated. After a number of fish are caught, the ring is removed and the Cormorant is allowed to fish for his own dinner.

Cormorants are very common along Florida beaches. They love to squabble over choice pilings. They sit lined up on old docks, piers, and especially channel markers.

COOTS and DUCKS

There are 20 to 30 varieties of ducks that visit Florida each year. It is beyond the scope of this book to show them all, so some of the more common are included here.

▶ The American Coot is often mistaken for a duck, but is actually a member of the Rail family. It has unusual, large, lobed feet, which are useful for paddling and running across the surface of ponds to reach takeoff speed.

▶ Large flocks of Scaup ducks are common on Florida bays in winter. Look for the black markings, front and rear.

▲ The Mallard is the one duck most people recognize on sight. This is the familiar green-headed male Mallard (drake) with the female (hen) behind.

▲ Any duck that has this colorful, fleshy growth around the face is a Muscovy. The body may be black, white, or mixed color. They tend to outproduce other waterbirds and take over available space in a pond.

This is a goose herding young ducks in a motherly way. It may be that she is watching over these ducks because she has lost her own babies. These fowl are domestic varieties that have become semi-wild and are commonly seen on Florida lakes and ponds. They are favorites with lakeside residents who tame and feed them.

EGRETS
Great Egret (American Egret)

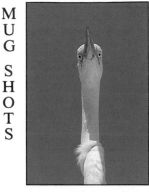

Front (fish's view)   Profile (human's view)

<u>Identification:</u> This very large white bird has jet-black legs and a yellow beak. It is so common, that most any tall white bird you see is probably a Great Egret (except in the Florida Keys where the Great White Heron is frequently seen). For positive identification, check leg and beak color.

▶ Breeding Plumage: During the nesting season, Great Egrets grow long feathers called "Aigrettes." The plumes grow from the upper back of the bird and are not tail feathers. The brilliant green color in front of the eyes (called the "loral area") is also part of the breeding season changes. In Snowy Egrets, this area becomes bright red.

Baby Egret in the nest.

Wading and fishing.

Feeding in the shallows of the bay at low tide.

The Plume Hunters

Around the turn of the Century, the fashion industry was using large quantities of plumes for ladies hats and accessories. The demand was so great that the price of plumes rose to over $30.00 per ounce, more than double the price of gold. The result of this irresistible lure was that hundreds of thousands of birds were slaughtered in Florida. The most efficient technique was to shoot them in their nesting areas. This resulted in the death of the babies and unhatched eggs as well. Other species (such as the Roseate Spoonbill) that did not produce valuable plumes, but nested in the same areas, were driven off by the carnage. Extinction of many waterbird species was a real threat until federal legislation combined with private pressure and money from groups like the National Audubon Society turned the tide. One Audubon warden guarding a private sanctuary lost his life in the brutal fight.

EGRETS
Cattle Egrets

Conquering the New World

These birds are natives of Africa and were unknown in the Americas until the 1930's when they suddenly appeared in South America. They had apparently flown across the Atlantic Ocean with the help of strong tail winds. By the 1950's they had appeared in Florida and now are a very common sight throughout this state and much of Eastern United States.

Cattle Egrets wade in water like other Egrets, but they have their own unique feeding system. They are most frequently seen in pastures around cattle. They follow the animals through the grass. The movement of the large beasts stirs up insects which are eaten by the Cattle Egrets. They also are known to follow farm machinery for the same purpose. Of all the birds in this book, the Cattle Egret is the least dependent upon water creatures for its food supply.

▼ In breeding plumage, the Cattle Egret develops a striking brown buff color on the head, back and the chest.

EGRETS
Reddish Egret

This beautiful, but uncommon Egret "comes in two colors": white and dark. The dark type appears more frequently in Florida, while the white appears more often along the Texas coast. The pink bill with black tip is brightest in color during the breeding season.

Immature Reddish Egret

Canopy Feeding ▲

The Reddish Egret can be spotted at a distance by his special fishing technique. He spreads his wings, creating shadows on the water. Small fish are attracted to hide in these dark spots and the Reddish Egret reaps his reward.

▼ Territorial dispute between Reddish Egret males is settled in an ancient manner.

Florida's "Color Morph" Birds

Some species of birds, such as the Reddish Egret, exist in two completely different colors. They do not change from one color to the other in a life cycle (like, for instance, the Little Blue Heron), but remain the same color throughout their lives.

Scientifically, this is called "dimorphism" meaning "two forms." Dimorphic forms of birds are not hybrids, since hybrids result from the cross of two different species.

These "birds of a different color" may breed together and do create some mixed offspring. In spite of interbreeding, the Reddish Egret remains basically either white or dark.

Another Florida bird that shows the "color morph" phenomenon is the Great Blue Heron. This species includes the Great White Heron and Würdemann's Heron. These three Herons are very much alike except for color.

EGRETS
Snowy Egrets

The Snowy Egret feeds with quick sprints through the water to stir up fish and then lightning jabs to grasp its meal.

▶ Snowy Egrets are common around fishing piers and can become rather tame. This little bird balanced on a boat mooring line. Each time the rocking boat moved toward the dock, the rope would slacken and lower the bird close enough to the water so that he could grab a small fish before he was hoisted up again.

◀ This is not a tightrope balancing act, but a chase scene. Note the crest of feathers on the head of the bird on the right. They are raised as a threat because the other bird has entered his territory.

Golden Slippers

This bird's most striking feature is its beautiful pair of bright yellow feet. The solid black beak is handy for identification if the feet are under water.

Breeding Plumage

FLAMINGO

▲ Eating and Squabbling. This photo shows the two most common daily activities of the captive Flamingo.

Flamingos have become a symbol of Florida, like the palm tree and the sunset, but they are most commonly seen at tourist attractions. Most of these birds were captured in the Caribbean Islands. There are a few small colonies in the wilds of the Everglades, but the casual observer can see many at close range at places like Tampa's Busch Gardens, and Miami's Hialeah Racetrack.

Captive Flamingos

Zoos and tourist attractions usually clip a small amount of bone from the end of one wing (called "pinioning"). This makes the birds too unstable in flight to go far and allows them to roam about freely without escaping.

Special chemicals are added to the Flamingos' diet so the birds will retain their beautiful pink color. This color fades rapidly in captivity when the Flamingo does not receive its usual natural diet of fresh seafood. At first, paprika and carrot byproducts were used, but now a more direct chemical has been found.

◀ Broken Legs? No, most birds sit this way. What appears to be a forward bending *knee* is actually the *ankle* in bird anatomy.

▶ The Flamingo possesses a truly unique beak which is bent at an angle to allow the bird to feed in a standing position with the head down and still scoop up and strain small creatures from the water.

FRIGATEBIRD
Magnificent Frigatebird

Female Frigatebirds have solid white breasts and black necks, while immature Frigatebirds have solid white heads.

This bird is usually seen as a dark silhouette, slowly soaring on air currents high in the summer sky above Florida beaches. Look for the forked tail. The graceful Frigatebird usually flies with his tail open in a "Y" shape, but sometimes the two sides are held together in a single point.

The male Frigatebird has an amazing red pouch which can be puffed out to the size of a football during courtship to attract a female. This pouch is not inflated at other times.

The Frigatebird spends much of its life in the air. Its huge wingspan makes it difficult to take off from the ground or the water, so most flights begin and end at the top of a tall tree. Once airborne, few birds can match its ability to fly.

The Frigatebird is sometimes called a "Man-O-War" because it attacks other birds, such as gulls and terns, to steal food and nesting material. When not stealing food, it can obtain its own meals by swooping low to the water and grabbing fish near the surface with its long beak. Despite its reputation as a pirate, most of its food is legitimately earned in this manner.

GALLINULES
(Moorhen)

The Common Gallinule is a duck-like bird frequently seen on fresh water ponds where it swims with Coots (see Coot section for comparison). The red shield on the forehead makes it unmistakably different. It loves to climb on and around tall grass and reeds at the edge of lakes.

▼ The Purple Gallinule is one of the most beautiful birds in the world. It has the intense bluish purple of a peacock on its chest and a light blue shield on its forehead. Its legs are bright yellow with extremely large feet which allow it to walk on lilly pads and other water plants in search of insect food.

◄ The pond at Royal Palm in the Florida Everglades National Park is the best place to look for this bird. Unlike the Common Gallinules, which are extremely numerous and can be seen on most Florida lakes, the Purple Gallinule is a rare and exciting find.

GULLS Laughing Gull

No Seagulls

Scientifically, there is no such species as "Seagull" and some dictionaries do not include the word. Nevertheless, it is very commonly used as a catch-all name for the many different kinds of Gulls. The Gulls most frequently found in Florida are shown here.

The old professor was asked by his students about "Seagulls." Scratching his head, he replied, "I don't know about 'C-Gulls' or 'D-Gulls,' but the 'E-Gull' is our national bird."

Brown and White Gulls

Notice that regardless of the type of Gull, the immature birds have brown bodies while the bodies of the adult birds are white.

Watch for this!

Gulls will open stubborn shellfish by carrying them to great heights land then dropping them. This behavior seems instinctive, but Laughing Gulls do learn by trial and error to drop the shellfish on a hard surface rather than a soft beach.

GULLS Laughing Gulls

Laughing Gull
summer plumage

Laughing Gulls, like most other birds, scoop up fresh drinking water using the lower beak like a spoon.

Laughing Gulls feeding on a wave crest. They grab tiny fish from the water while in flight, but do not dive into the water like the terns.

GULLS
Ring-billed Gull

Florida's Gulls are not all the same size. Laughing Gulls are among the smallest with the Ring-billed Gull the next size larger. Herring Gulls and Black-backed Gulls are the jumbo size birds.

Ring-bills, like the other Gulls, tend to flock together in groups of their own kind. Large numbers arrive in Florida in October and stay for the winter. Some Ring-bills remain all year.

Herring Gull—Adult

Herring Gull and Black-backed Gull

Both are large birds, considerably huskier than the other Gulls. They both have a red spot on the bottom halves of their beaks. This is believed to be a target that aids youngsters in the nest to peck at their parents when demanding food.

Herring Gull—Immature

Black-backed Gull

HERONS
Great Blue Heron

Adult

Immature

Adult:
Breeding Plumage

This hungry baby Heron in the nest is anxiously awaiting the arrival of his dinner. When the parent who has been out fishing finally returns, a beautiful ritual is performed by the mated pair. Bowing, stretching and wing spreading all accompany this changing of the guard. Students of bird behavior call the display a "Nest Relief Ceremony."

▲ This Heron is not just "blowin' in the wind," but is "shaking out" his rumpled feathers to align them for flight.

▲ Herons in flight extend their necks for takeoff, but they are quickly drawn back against their bodies in a folded "S" shape.

▲ "What's going on around here? Why are all these little sandpipers sneaking up on me?"

HERONS
Louisiana Heron (Tricolored)

▲ The Louisiana Heron does not swim, but sometimes wades in deep water.

◄ Immature Louisiana Heron peers through the grasses.

▶ "Too much thinking can make your brain itch."

Audubon called this bird "Lady of the Waters" because of its grace and beauty. This Heron is quite common, but the name, Louisiana Heron, is very misleading. It does occur in Louisiana, but also in the other coastal states from North Carolina to Texas, and especially in Florida.

It somewhat resembles the Great Blue Heron, but it is much smaller and more delicate. Its white belly clearly distinguishes it from all other Herons.

The Louisiana Heron fishes by striding briskly through the water, sometimes even running after fish which are caught with a quick thrust of the beak into the water. This move is so fast that it will blur a photograph taken at 1/1000 second shutter speed. A shutter speed of 1/4000 will stop a bullet.

"Save Film": Photograph these birds on calm waters and get two images for the price of one.

▲ The Louisiana Heron has a white patch on its back which makes identification from the rear easy.

HERONS
Little Blue Herons

The Little Blue Heron has a remarkable life cycle. It spends the first part of its life as a completely white bird. Next, it becomes a mottled color for a short while. Then, finally, it turns dark blue, the color it retains for the rest of its life.

Look for the bluish-beak with the black tip for positive identification.

"A hunting we will go. . ."

"What could be nicer for dinner than a . . ."

". . . crayfish and lettuce sandwich!"

HERONS
Great White Heron

The Great White Heron has pure white plumage and light colored legs which distinguish it from the Great Egret which has black legs. The "Great White" is a color phase of the Great Blue Heron (see discussion of color phases under "Reddish Egret").

It is rare to see this bird except in the Florida Keys or at the town of Flamingo in the Everglades National Park. In the Keys they are a very familiar sight.

This very limited range means small total numbers. Their population has been dangerously reduced at times by large hurricanes. The Great White Heron National Refuge in the Keys has been created for their protection.

HERONS
Night Herons

There are two kinds of Night Herons in Florida: Yellow-crowned, and Black-crowned. The Yellow-crowned, shown above, is common in Florida and will be seen feeding in the shallows by anyone who spends much time around the bays and inland waterways.

The Black-crowned is very common world-wide, but rare in Florida.

Night Shift Worker

Like his name implies, this Heron works at night, and thus avoids traffic jams with other birds who might be fishing in the same territory.

He must also be a workaholic because he is frequently seen in the daytime. Actually, the tides are more important to this bird than the position of the sun because he must have shallow water for wading.

▲ The threat display of the Yellow-crowned Night Heron consists of extending the neck, puffing the feathers, and raising the plumes on the top of the head. (These long feathers are called "nuchal plumes")

▲ Immature Yellow-crowned with crab.

◄► The Black-crowned Night Heron is a larger, much stockier bird which has a spectacular white plume on its head.

HERONS
Little Green Heron
(Green-backed Heron)

▲ This is a shy and very low profile bird. He favors swampy areas and the grassy edges of lakes. He does appear along the coast, but while the Great Blue Heron will stand on top of a dock and walk along the top of a seawall, the Little Green Heron will hide under the dock, and walk along the bottom of the seawall, out of human sight whenever possible.

▲ This Little Green Heron must have thought he was all alone because making a public appearance is not his style. Exhibitionism like this is out of the question.

▲ Patience is his virtue and the key to his fishing technique. He will find a branch overhanging the water and wait for the right moment to strike. He may also enter the water and stand motionless for many minutes. His bright yellow legs may attract fish.

An extraordinary feature of this bird is his ability to contract his neck so much that it appears his head grows directly on his shoulders. Or, he may extend his neck to almost unbelievable lengths.

This stretching motion is probably used to help move a large fish through his digestive tract. It is the bird equivalent of taking Rolaids. It is known to animal behavior scientists as a "comfort movement."

These baby Little Green Herons are attempting to hide from the photographer by raising their necks, remaining motionless, and pretending to be twigs on the branch.

HERONS
Würdemann's Heron

This beautiful creature exists only in the Florida Keys and in very limited numbers.

Würdemann's Heron was named for Gustavus Würdemann who was a collector for the Smithsonian Institute in the 1850's. At this time the bird was thought to be a separate species from the Great Blue Heron. The American Ornithologists Union (AOU) is the final judge of bird classification in scientific circles. They recently decided against a separate species for this bird (although not without some dissent). Würdemann's Heron is now considered just another color form of the Great Blue Heron.

This decision has angered some of the more competitive bird watchers who strive to add the most species possible to the "lifetime lists" of birds they have seen. Since this bird is no longer a separate species, it is one less triumph to be recorded by those who have seen it.

Through it all, this Würdemann's Heron remains unperturbed by the commotion he has caused and seems content to catch his daily fish and beg what he can from local fishermen. Most of the people on the bridges, are, likewise, unaware of the importance of this bird and treat him just like any other Heron, giving him the small fish and perhaps remarking about the dazzling pure white head of this otherwise grey-blue bird.

IBIS
White Ibis

Ibis are distinctive for their long, curving bill which turns a brilliant red during breeding season and contrasts with their beautiful blue eye color. The downward curving bill is called "decurved" in scientific language.

The Ibis roosts in large colonies in the mangrove forest along the coasts, or with Herons and Egrets at large inland roosts. They can be recognized in flight by their outstretched necks and black markings on their wingtips.

This bird was once hunted extensively for food by the Indians and early settlers and was said to taste like chicken. It is now protected by law like other wild birds.

The Sacred Ibis

The Egyptians regarded their Ibis with reverence because they believed that one of their Gods, Thoth, came to earth on occasion and assumed the form of an Ibis. This is a photo of an Ibis statue created by the ancient Egyptians and now on display at the Metropolitan Museum of Art in New York City. It is hollow inside and the body of a real Ibis was placed within.

▼ The Glossy Ibis can be seen in the central part of the state on the wet prairies, but is much less common along the coast.

▼ The Scarlet Ibis is common in South America and an occasional bird is reported in Florida. These may have escaped from zoos or attractions.

Immature White Ibis

Adult White Ibis

KINGFISHER
Belted Kingfisher

If "Eternal vigilance is the price of liberty," then, surely, this bird will remain forever free. Of all the birds in this book, the Kingfisher gets the prize for general wariness, suspicion, and downright paranoia.

The bird lover who tries to approach this perky species will be treated to a show of tailfeathers sandwiched between a pair of pounding wings.

Notice the dark band across the chest from which the "Belted" Kingfisher derives its name. Females have a second "belt" of brownish color across the stomach. Both male and female have the showy crest of feathers on the head which can be raised when the bird is alarmed.

▶ Throughout Florida these birds are perched on phone wires and branches overlooking water. The Kingfisher spots a fish, flies out to a spot directly above his prey, hovers, then plunges straight down into the water. He usually flies back to his perch with a fish in his mouth.

This bird usually fishes alone and is not seen in flocks or even with a mate except during the breeding season. Its territory is usually small and fiercely defended against other Kingfishers. Most birds use the same few perches every day. Many persons in Florida who have a waterfront home and boat dock also have a resident Kingfisher who uses the dock as his perch.

◀ The Kingfisher nests by digging a horizontal burrow several feet deep into the dirt bank of a ditch or stream and there, in a cave-like environment, raises its young. A burrow of this size can take weeks to dig.

In some parts of the country, such as southern Florida, the ground is flat and it is difficult to find a stream with steep enough banks to dig a decent burrow. In this case, the Kingfisher may use a hollow tree as a substitute homesite.

LIMPKIN

The Limpkin is a large, slow moving bird of the deep swamp, best seen in the dim light of early morning, late afternoon, or cloudy days. Its dinner is mostly freshwater snails which it collects from the stems and leaves of plants.

The name comes from its slow, crippled appearance when walking. It is also famed for its terrifying screams in the middle of the night.

The Limpkin's beak is specially adapted for prying snails out of their shells.

OSPREY

The Osprey is a large, fish-eating bird of prey, that is frequently mistaken for a Bald Eagle because of its white head. At close range or with binoculars, it can be seen that the Osprey has a dark band across its face and a smaller, less colorful beak than his more famous relative. Even more obvious is the white breast. Eagles are dark underneath.

Ospreys build large nests which they expand and improve year after year. Some of these can be seen along the causeway to the Florida Keys. Most nests are built in tall trees, but the Osprey is adaptable and will use man made structures such as phone poles. This bird co-exists well with man and seems unconcerned about cars and people.

The Osprey's foot is very rough textured for grasping slippery prey. The Osprey is the only hawk able to grasp with two toes in front and two in back rather than the usual three and one arrangement.

"Got a Hold on You"

The Osprey plunges feet first into the water and grabs his fish with the sharp claws. Sometimes, when a fish is too big to carry, the Osprey is unable to let go. One theory is that the excitement of the catch stimulates a locking mechanism. Some people believe the claws simply sink into bone and get stuck.

Whatever the reason, fishermen have caught large fish with Osprey feet attached. These unfortunate birds perished by the same unique ability that enables them to survive.

PELICANS
Brown Pelican

The Brown Pelican is a favorite of the locals and the darling of the tourists. He is one of the most fascinating of Florida's waterbirds, and no doubt, the most popular.

One reason may be that the Pelican is playful. He has a lot of personality and never seems quite so serious as the other birds. His yawns and stretches are a comic joy to watch. He has time for fun, and, he will do *anything* for a fish.

Here, then, is that master entertainer, the jester of the waterfront, Florida's "Clown Prince," the Brown Pelican.

▲ Soaring along the coast, the Brown Pelican spots his prey. Banking out of the sky in a steep climbing turn, the big bird stalls in flight, and drops like a rock.

▲ Wings are set to give final course corrections.

▲ The Pelican is then ready to swallow his catch and take off. At this moment Gulls may attempt to steal the food and sometimes they succeed. They are brazen enough at times to even sit on the Pelican's head and wait for a chance to grab his fish.

THE
DIVE

▶ At impact, the wings are folded back out of the way and the bird has flipped over.

▶ Pelicans have special air sacks under their flesh on the front of the body to cushion them from the constant pounding against the water surface.

▲ The Pelican does not spear his catch, but rather, uses his pouch like a fishnet. The lower beak, normally long and narrow, stretches out wide under water to almost the shape of a basketball hoop. Upon surfacing, the pouch is tilted forward and drained.

▲ The tremendous impact with the water stuns the fish.

In the Nest

▲ Male Pelican offers nesting material to the female. Notice this view of Pelican feet which shows the toes and webbing pointing inward.

Small Territories

▶ Pelican nests are built close together in low trees or mangroves. The birds will snap their beaks at intruders, but will only defend an area that is the distance they can reach when sitting in the nest.

▶ Pelican babies are born without feathers and are fed partially digested fish from the parent's gullet.

Usually, two or three chicks are hatched. Each hatching is two days apart. It is a sad fact that the first chick and sometimes the second chick, have such a head start in growth that they can grab all the food. This means the smallest bird sometimes starves to death.

▲ As the Pelican baby grows larger, he can reach into the parent's gullet and obtain his own food.

▲ Four or five times a day these youngsters will demand a feeding. The parents comply whenever possible.

▲ All is domestic tranquility until the parent spots an intruder and issues a threat in defense of the jumbo-size baby.

▶ These chicks are about five weeks old and have fluffy down coats. They will be ready to leave the nest at twelve weeks.

Boaters passing close to Pelicans nesting in the mangroves should use extreme caution. If the chicks become excited and fall from the nest, the parents will not retrieve them, and they will perish.

PELICAN PLUMAGE CHANGES

▲ <u>First year Pelican</u> has a brown colored neck and wings. The belly is very white.

▲ <u>Second year Pelican</u> is more grey than brown. The neck is starting to turn light and the belly has some dark feathers.

Male and Female

▲ Here is the only noticeable difference. The male bird on the left has a slightly longer beak. The bird with the shorter beak on the right is female. In this picture the male is a second year bird while the female is first year.

▲ <u>Adult Pelican-Summer Plumage</u>. By the third year, the adult pelican's belly is quite dark. In the summertime, the head is white with a dark brown stripe on the back of the neck.

In this photo a clear membrane covers the pelican's eyeball. This is called the "nictitating membrane" and protects the eye in flight and under water. This bird has blinked it shut just for a moment. It is usually open when the bird is safely perched.

<u>Adult Pelican-Winter Plumage</u>.
◄ In early fall, the brown stripe molts to white and yellow plumage appears on the head. This lasts until nesting has begun in Spring. The yellow head is basically a courting plumage.

<u>Adult Pelican-Winter Changing to Summer Plumage</u>.
► There is a period of about one month in the Spring when the white neck molts to dark brown and the yellow head has not yet changed to pure white.

Pelican Flight

Watch for this

Pelicans frequently fly together in long lines of several or more birds. They will flap their wings and then glide. The flaps are not at the same moment, but in sequence, starting with the leader. Each bird will flap when he reaches the same spot where the lead bird began to flap.

▶ Pelicans take off from the water with an assist from their feet. Both feet are kicked together to boost the large body into the air.

◀ Pelican soaring is a very beautiful sight. Frequently, the birds will fly only inches above the water.

▶ Landings in the water are accomplished with both feet out front, skidding against the water as brakes.

Around the Fishing Pier

▶ The Problem: Pelicans frequently get tangled in hooks and fishing line.

If the line is cut by the fisherman and remains dangling from the bird, it will get caught in the mangrove tree roost and the bird will starve. If it wraps around a foot or wing, circulation will be stopped and the limb lost.

Pelicans and Fishermen

Some fishermen dislike Pelicans because they feel the birds are competing with them. Actually, Pelicans only hunt for small bait fish. When they are seen with larger fish, it is usually the gift of a fisherman. The diving sequence on the previous page shows the typical 6″ to 8″ catch.

Acts of extreme cruelty against the birds have occurred. Fortunately, most fishermen truly enjoy the Pelicans because of the entertainment they offer.

In the wintertime, fish swim deeper where the Pelicans cannot catch them and many birds go hungry. They are very grateful for the generosity of those fishermen and others who help them through this season with handouts.

▼ How To Help: If a bird is hooked, it should be slowly reeled in. From a pier, the bird can be lifted up with a net or walked to the shore. A Pelican on the dock can be tempted with a fish while someone sneaks up behind him, grabs his beak, and holds it. Pelicans are gentle, but the small hook on the tip of the bill can cause scratches when they are excited.

The bird's wings can be stretched out, preferably in a group effort, and hooks and line removed. Frequently, more than one hook will be found. A fishhook should be pushed through the skin, the barb cut off with wirecutters, and the hook backed out.

Seriously injured birds should be taken to bird hospitals (see last page). Deliberate abuse of birds is illegal and should be reported to the Florida Game and Freshwater Fish Commission or U.S. Fish and Wildlife Service.

◀ Although they do not hunt large fish, hungry Pelicans around the piers would try to swallow a whale if given the chance. Their close and friendly association with man leads to the problems shown above.

▲ Girl Watching? No, but there is a fish in the red bucket.

Question: Which of these men just caught a fish?

Pelicans Forever?

Brown Pelicans seem to be everywhere along the Florida coast, but in reality they are an Endangered Species.

Their strong presence in Florida is misleading. By the 1970's, the Brown Pelican had almost disappeared from California, Texas, and Louisiana, all states which formerly had heavy populations. The reason, many believe, was that pesticides had worked their way into the water, then to the fish, and finally, up the food chain to the Pelicans. These birds at the top of the food chain stored and concentrated the poisons in their bodies. The result was fatally thin egg shells.

After federal laws banned DDT in 1972, Pelicans started to make a slow comeback. Florida is the only area of the country where the Pelican had not suffered heavily from the poisons. Here he is now threatened with over-building and the resulting loss of nesting areas.

PELICANS
White Pelicans

The Brown Pelican is a year-round resident of Florida, but the White Pelican breeds in mountain lakes of northern states such as Montana and Utah during the summer months and then flies to Florida. Large flocks spend the winter at Florida Bay. The town of Flamingo in the Everglades National Park is a place where they can always be observed.

During the breeding season, the male White Pelican has a large, distinctive growth on the top of his bill. This growth may serve a function. During battles between Pelicans when rival birds snap at each other, this spot seems to be a target of some of the attacks. By drawing the fire in this manner, the peculiar growth may reduce more dangerous stabs at the soft and easily torn pouch.

White Pelicans do not dive for their food like Brown Pelicans. Instead, they fish in large groups. The White Pelicans form a semi-circle of 10 or 15 birds and herd fish toward the shore. Then, while still swimming on the surface of the water, they use their pouches like fishnets and scoop up their prey.

Opposite Page: A pair of European White Pelicans demonstrate their affectionate nature. Compare their faces with those of the Florida White Pelicans.

SANDPIPERS
and Other Small Wading Birds

Sandpipers are some of the most frequently noticed waterbirds, and certainly they are among the most popular. Along with Pelicans and Gulls, they are always present along the beaches. There are many kinds of Sandpipers in Florida. Here are the ones you are most likely to see.

Sanderlings

Sanderlings may be the cutest of all the sandpipers because they are so small, run so fast, and always seem to be fleeing from crashing waves. They are easy to recognize by their pure white belly in the winter. In the summertime, they become rust colored.

Sanderlings breed in the Arctic in the Spring and then scatter so widely that they are found on almost every beach in the world.

Willet (or Won't It?)

The Willet stands out on the beaches because it is a very common year around resident in Florida and also because it is much larger than the other sandpipers.

In flight the Willet shows a distinct white patch on the wings. In the summer, a pattern of darker feathers appears on the Willet's chest.

Yellowlegs

The Yellowlegs is another relatively large Sandpiper, but not as large as the Willet. The bright yellow leg color makes identification easy. The bird shown at left is the "Greater Yellowlegs." There is also, as you might guess, a "Lesser Yellowlegs" shown below, which is a smaller bird with a shorter beak. The beak of the "Lesser" is straight. The beak of the "Greater" is slightly upturned.

Dowitcher

The Dowitcher stands out in a crowd because he has the longest straight bill of all the Sandpipers. It is very useful for probing deeply into the ground on mudflats and edges of ponds. There is a "Short-billed Dowitcher," as shown in the photos, and also a "Long-billed Dowitcher." Both have very long bills and are hard to tell apart. Dowitchers are brownish in the Summer, as in the photos, and grey-colorless in the Winter.

Ruddy Turnstone

The Ruddy Turnstone is well named. He has reddish legs and is known for turning over every stone and shell on the beach in his search for food. He is usually found on the type of beach that has lots of rocks and seaweed.

Red Knots

▶ These birds are long distance migrants. They breed in the Arctic in the summer and then most of them fly to Argentina for the winter. A portion (perhaps the lazy ones) don't bother to make this long journey. They stop off in Florida from September to March before returning to the Arctic breeding grounds. Although brownish red in summer, they are usually seen in their grey winter plumage when in Florida.

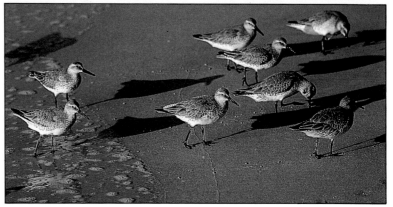

Dunlin

◀ The Dunlin resembles the Dowitcher, but does not have the ultra-long beak. Also, the Dunlin's beak is curved downward at the tip. In the summer, this bird also breeds in the Arctic.

Plover

▼ The most common types in Florida are the Black-bellied Plover which has a jet black belly in summer plumage, and the Semipalmated which is smaller and is distinguished by the single dark band across its chest. Plovers have beaks which are shorter than Sandpipers and bulge to a greater thickness at the tip.

Semipalmated

Least Sandpiper

▲ This bird is recognized by its extremely small size and its light colored, yellowish legs.

Black-necked Stilt

This bird is amazing for the slenderness of its legs and beak. However, these features give him the advantage of being able to wade and feed in deeper water than a number of other birds that might compete for the same food. The Stilt is a true sky-scraper in comparison with the other birds in this section. A full sized adult bird may stand over 15 inches tall.

He is most likely to be seen around Lake Okeechobee or in the Central Florida vegetable fields when they are flooded in the summer to kill insect pests. The Stilt does appear in coastal areas such as Sanibel Island, but seems to prefer wet pastures such as the Kissimmee Prairie north of Lake Okeechobee.

Stilts hunt a wide variety of water creatures. While they do catch small fish, the bulk of their diet consists of various water bugs and larvae.

American Oystercatcher

The most amazing feature of this bird, of course, is the bright red bill which is flat on both sides and used skillfully to pry open shellfish. It is also poked into the mud to grasp deeply buried prey and can be used to wedge free various shellfish that attach themselves to rocks.

The bright bill is a liability at nesting time because, rather than camouflage, it acts like a beacon for any predators. Because of this, the Oystercatcher will put on a broken wing act to lure animals away from its eggs, which, when left alone, are well camouflaged to resemble the rocky beaches on which they are laid.

"Hello"

"Goodby"

SKIMMERS
Black Skimmers

▲ Dead bird? No, just a Black Skimmer resting on a warm asphalt parking lot.

▲ The immature Skimmer lacks the jet-black wing feathers of the adult.

▲ This is what a Skimmer's wet tail feathers look like after the bird has been fishing all day.

▲ Skimmers like to nest on sand bars and causeways, sometimes dangerously close to people and traffic. They return to the same sites every year. Since they are very vulnerable in some places, the Florida Wildlife officers put up ropes and markers to keep people from disturbing them.

▲ This bird is getting too big for the nest, but still wants to hide from the sun under its parent. Skimmers have vertical slit eye pupils which reduce the harsh glare from the white sand.

This fascinating bird has special feeding skills and equipment. The adult skimmer develops a lower beak which is much longer than the upper beak. This long lower beak is dragged through the water to catch food.

Skimmers are most commonly seen fishing along the edge of beaches and bays at dusk and have no trouble fishing after the sun has set. In fact, they prefer night fishing because the water is generally calmer and there are more fish near the surface.

▼ Skimmers at rest on the beaches, like most shorebirds, will line up facing into the wind. When airborne in groups, they are capable of beautiful synchronized flight, rising and turning together with perfect coordination.

SPOONBILLS
Roseate Spoonbill

The Spoonbill is one of Florida's most colorful birds. Although it is not common everywhere in the state, if you visit the wildlife refuges on Sanibel Island or Merritt Island, you will surely see them.

Carrying nesting material.

Florida's Pink Birds

Most Florida visitors are not familiar with Spoonbills. The first time they see this large pink wader from a distance, they are sure they are looking at a Flamingo.

The Flamingo is much taller, and has an angled beak rather than the very flat, spoon-shaped beak of the Spoonbill.

Sleeping.

▲ The adult birds have beautiful ruby red eyes and bald heads. Immature birds have dark brown eyes and are not as pink.

▶ Spoonbills feed by swinging their beaks from side to side through the water. When a special nerve ending in the beak signals contact with food, the beak instantly closes.

STORKS
Wood Stork

Also known as "Wood Ibis," "Ironhead," or "Flinthead," this bird is the only Stork in the United States. The bald head and neck give him a very strange appearance. The beak in the photo at left is rather shabby looking because a Stork's beak (like the beaks of many other birds) has an outer layer that peels off at regular intervals.

Wood Storks are very "colonial" birds. Of course, "colonial" does not mean that they come from Merry Old England to establish an empire. In the "birders" use of the word, it means that they like to nest in the company of other Storks. Wood Storks also like to roost together and feed together.

◄ In spite of the Wood Stork's awkward appearance, he is graceful in the air. Storks fly with neck outstretched and show large black areas under the wings.

▲ Fish are caught by walking slowly through muddy water with beak submerged, waiting for fish to make contact. The fish is grabbed and swallowed the moment it is detected. The reaction time is amazingly short. In fact, the closing of a Stork's beak is considered one of the fastest movements in the animal kingdom.

▼ After feeding, Wood Storks do a lot standing around, but they do it with a certain style. It is this dignified manner and solemn personality that has earned them the nickname "Preacherbirds."

Successful breeding by Wood Storks re-
quires large amounts of food. Since Wood
Storks fish by feel and not by sight, fish must
be present in large concentrations.

In the Everglades and parts of South
Florida where these birds live, winter is the dry
season. Water holes become smaller. The fish
are then closely packed and feeding is easy.

When the rain and drought cycle does not
occur on schedule, or when the flow of water
to the grasslands is disrupted by man's
agricultural uses, very little breeding occurs.
Plentiful food supplies must be present in time
to match the Wood Storks breeding efforts. In
recent years, this has not occurred.

The population of Wood Storks is not
large enough to survive continually poor
breeding seasons. Thus, without some
cooperation from man, this bird is in danger.

A Wood Stork "chorus line"

TERNS

Gulls and Terns Compared

Terns are frequently confused with Gulls. Here is a simple way to tell the difference.

The photo at right shows the Gull to be a much larger bird than the Forster's Tern. Terns are faster, have forked tails, pointed beaks, and a longer, more streamlined body shape.

Terns swoop down and grab small fish from the water, but seldom sit on the water like gulls. It is common to see Terns hover in the air for quite some time, then dive straight down into the water. They grab the fish and are airborne again.

Royal Tern

This Tern has a beautiful orange beak and perky looking tuft of black feathers on the back of the head. Like other Terns, they frequently flock together in large groups on sandbars and beaches.

Common Tern

◄ This Common Tern shows winter plumage. In the summer, the top of the head will become solid black and the beak will have some reddish color.

Sandwich Tern

▶ Note the "mayonnaise" on the tip of the bill. This yellow tip makes the Sandwich Tern stand out.

Brown Noddy

Noddy Tern and Sooty Tern

◀▼ These two Terns are part of the natural beauty of the Dry Tortugas Islands. The Tortugas are located a short plane ride from Key West.

There is an old federal fort which can be visited. It is famous as the prison that held Dr. Mudd, the physician who set the broken leg of John Wilkes Booth, President Lincoln's assassin.

Sooty Tern

American Bittern

◀ This is a very shy bird you will not be likely to see because he is always hiding. That's why he is hiding at the end of this book among the Terns instead of being back in the Heron section where he belongs.

The Bittern spends its time in the tall grasses of swamps and ponds. He blends in perfectly. He is so confident of his camouflage that he will sometimes not move even when humans approach to within a few feet. By lifting his head and swaying in perfect rhythm as winds move the grasses, this bird "just plain disappears."

Bitterns use their voices to communicate with other Bitterns to find a mate. Vision is limited in the tall grass, even for these birds.

White Pelicans

SAVING THE BIRDS
SUNCOAST SEABIRD SANCTUARY

Feeding hungry pelicans on the beach during winter food shortage.

Ralph Heath, Jr., Sanctuary founder.

Are Injured Birds Worthless?

Many people would think so, and might believe they should be destroyed, but Ralph Heath, Jr. has been changing some minds. He created the Suncoast Seabird Sanctuary because of compassion for a wounded bird, but has developed it into a center for research, education, and captive breeding of endangered species such as the Brown Pelican.

Permanently injured pelicans that would not survive in the wild are nursed back to health and allowed to live out their lives at the Sanctuary. They have fledged large numbers of babies while providing first hand knowledge and enjoyment to thousands of visitors. Injured birds that are treated here and cannot be released have found homes at zoos and tourist attractions around the world. This is an ideal place to study many water-birds at close range. The Sanctuary is on the beach at Indian Shores between St. Petersburg and Clearwater. Admission is free. Contributions are appreciated.